D0604495

TETON COUNTY LIBRARY
JACKSON, WYOMING

Thanks to Frances Perkins

Fighter for Workers' Rights

With thanks to the Peachtree team, especially Kathy and Margaret, who have done so much to bring stories like this to life —D. H.

To Rumi, with thanks —K. C.

Published by
PEACHTREE PUBLISHING COMPANY INC.
1700 Chattahoochee Avenue
Atlanta, Georgia 30318-2112
www.peachtree-online.com

Text © 2020 by Deborah Hopkinson
Illustrations © 2020 by Kristy Caldwell

All rights reserved. No part of this publication may be reproduced, stored in a retrieval system, or transmitted in any form or by any means—electronic, mechanical, photocopy, recording, or any other—except for brief quotations in printed reviews, without the prior permission of the publisher.

Edited by Kathy Landwehr
Design and composition by Kristy Caldwell and Adela Pons
The illustrations were rendered digitally.

Printed in March 2020 by Toppan Leefung Printing Limited in China
10 9 8 7 6 5 4 3 2 1
First Edition
ISBN 978-1-68263-136-2

Cataloging-in-Publication Data is available from the Library of Congress.

Acknowledgments

Special thanks to Princeton Williams, Senior Outreach Program Manager, Public Affairs, Federal Reserve Bank of Atlanta, and to Dr. Erin Yetter, University of Arizona, for their careful reading of the manuscript.

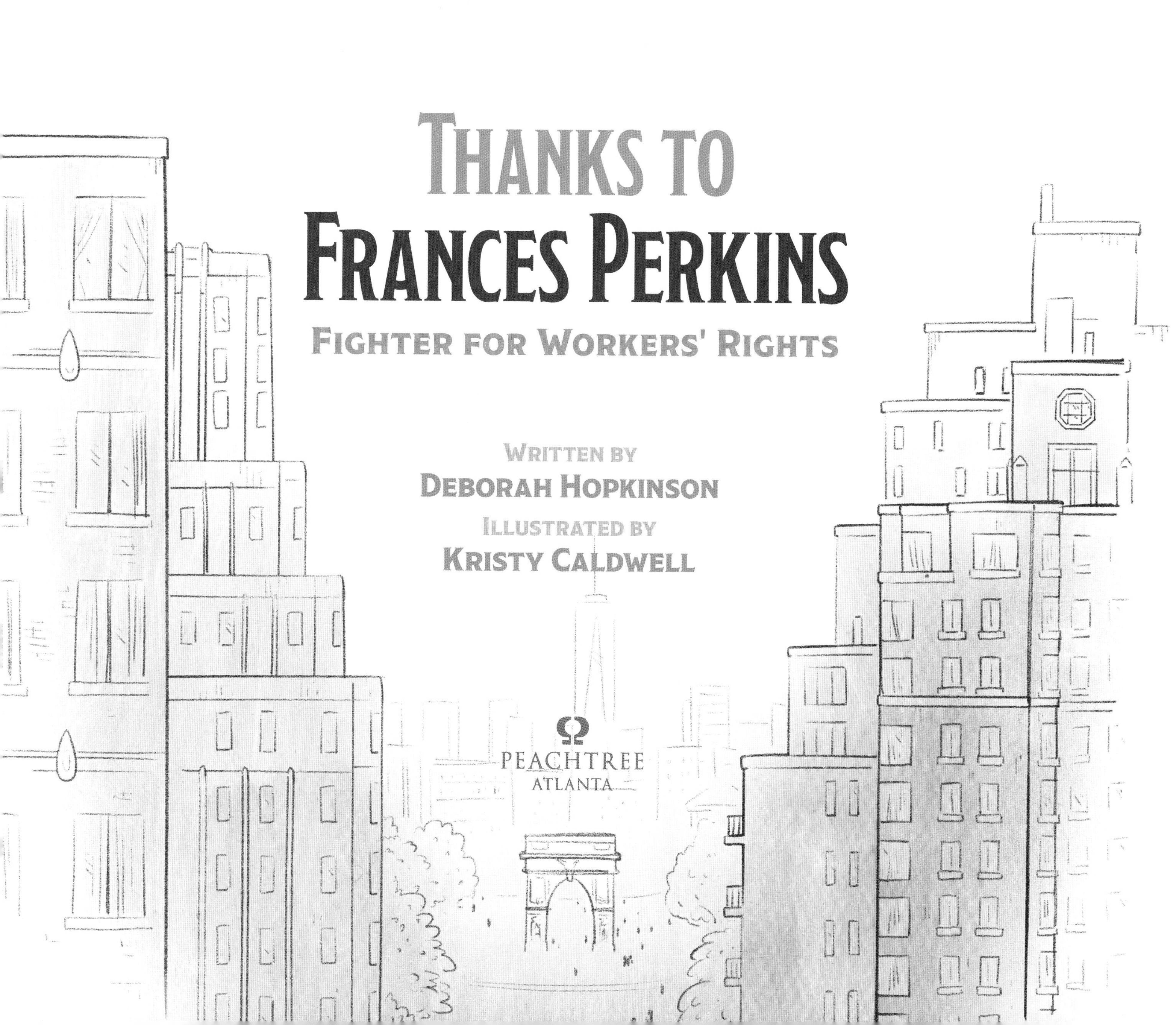

Thanks to Frances Perkins

Fighter for Workers' Rights

Written by
Deborah Hopkinson
Illustrated by
Kristy Caldwell

Peachtree
Atlanta

Let's start with two math questions, especially for you younger readers.

1. How many years will it be until you turn sixty-two?
2. What year will that be?

Now, hold onto your answers until the end, when you'll find out why this is important.

And why (when you get there) you'll want to thank Frances Perkins.

Frances was born in 1880 in Boston.

Her father believed in education.

Her mother taught her to help neighbors in need.

And her wise grandmother said that whenever a door of opportunity opened, Frances should go through.

Perhaps that's why Frances grew up trusting in both her heart and her mind.

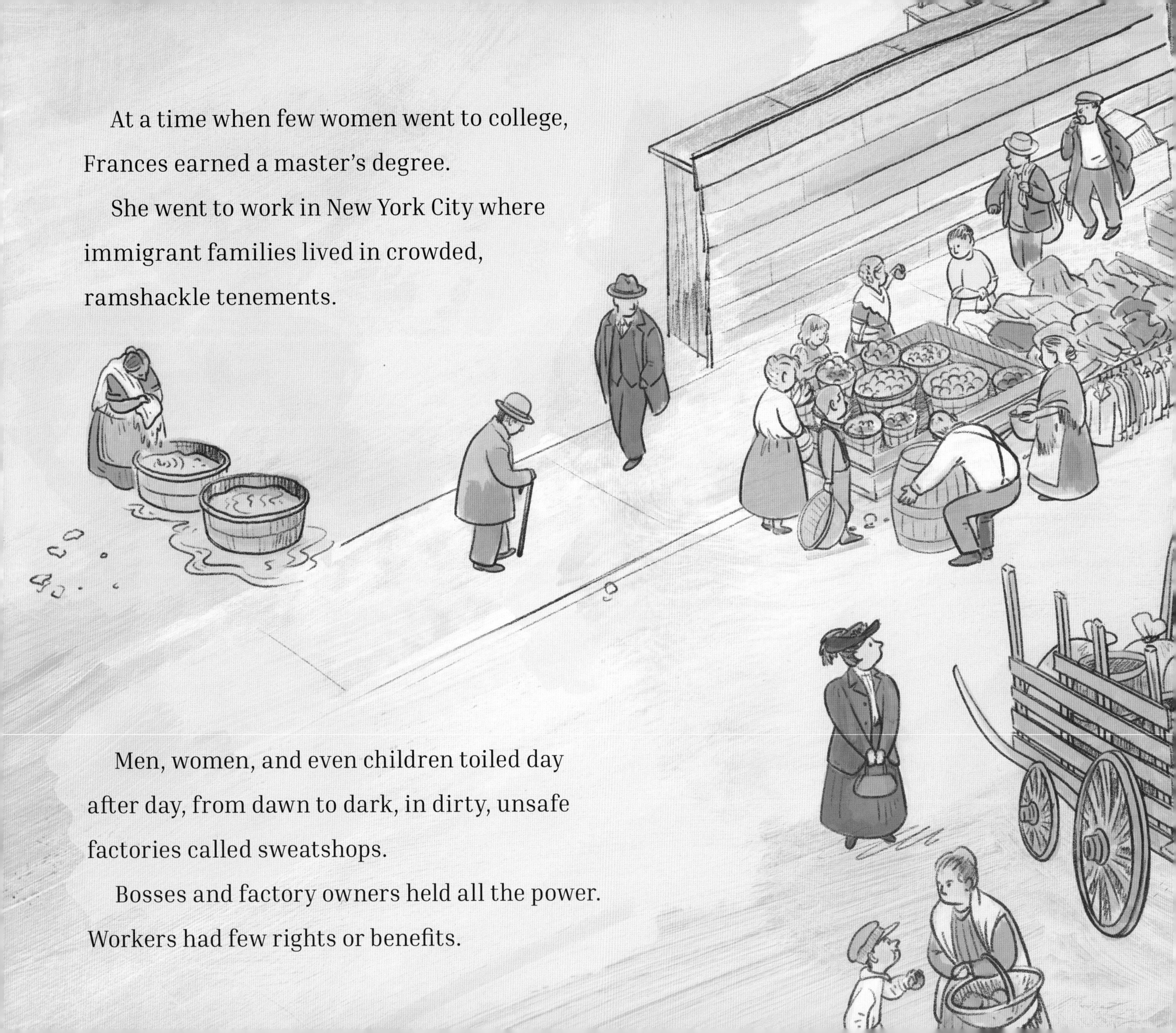

At a time when few women went to college, Frances earned a master's degree.

She went to work in New York City where immigrant families lived in crowded, ramshackle tenements.

Men, women, and even children toiled day after day, from dawn to dark, in dirty, unsafe factories called sweatshops.

Bosses and factory owners held all the power. Workers had few rights or benefits.

On Saturday, March 25, 1911, Frances witnessed a terrible tragedy.

While having tea with a friend in Washington Square, Frances heard fire whistles and shouts. She rushed outside. She saw flames pouring from high up in the Triangle Waist Company building where young women sewed white blouses called shirtwaists.

When the fire broke out, the workers were trapped by locked doors. Some made it onto window ledges, but the firemen's nets weren't strong enough to catch those who jumped or fell.

One hundred and forty-six people, mostly teenage girls, perished in a tragedy that shocked the nation.

A week later, still heartbroken and stunned, Frances went to a memorial gathering where young labor activist Rose Schneiderman spoke.

Rose declared that the time had come for change. “Too much blood has been spilled,” she cried. Rose urged workers to unite in the fight for better conditions.

Frances was so moved by Rose's words, she decided to join the fight for justice too. She wanted to help make new laws, to force factory owners and employers to treat people better and make workplaces safer. So Frances went to work for a committee set up to improve safety—and to keep tragedies like the Triangle factory fire from ever happening again.

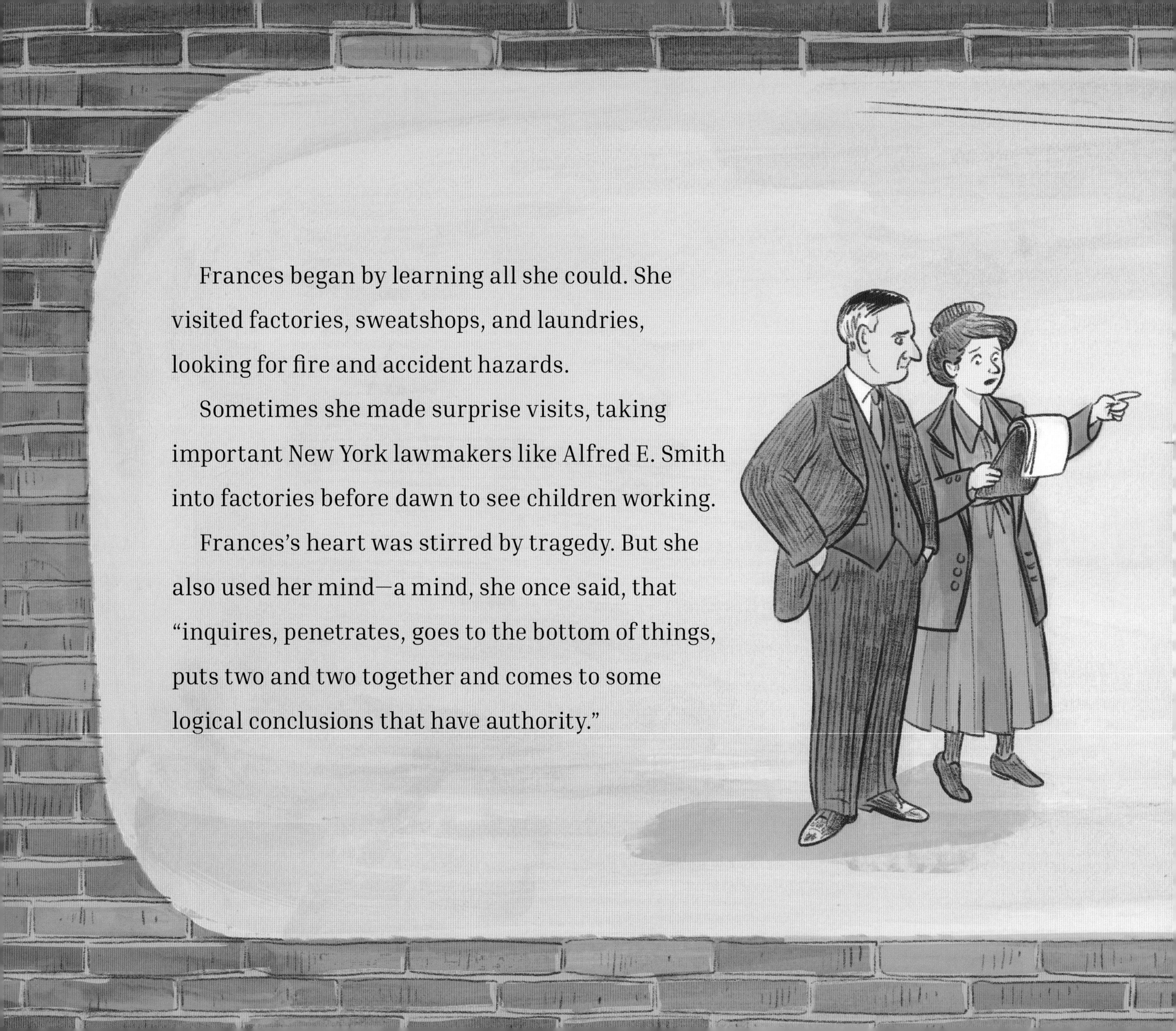

Frances began by learning all she could. She visited factories, sweatshops, and laundries, looking for fire and accident hazards.

Sometimes she made surprise visits, taking important New York lawmakers like Alfred E. Smith into factories before dawn to see children working.

Frances's heart was stirred by tragedy. But she also used her mind—a mind, she once said, that "inquires, penetrates, goes to the bottom of things, puts two and two together and comes to some logical conclusions that have authority."

And Frances *did* have authority. People listened to her, even though, in the halls of government and power, she was often the only woman.

She met with lawmakers, learned to persuade and compromise, and never gave up.

In 1912 Frances helped to get a bill passed to limit the work week to fifty-four hours for women and children under eighteen.

When she noticed how painful it was for women to sit for long hours on stools, she helped the workers get chairs with backs.

As more new laws to benefit workers came into being in New York, the state became a model for the nation. The changes Frances fought to bring about made all Americans more aware of the importance of social responsibility and the welfare of others.

It was, Frances said later, “a turning point.”

FIRE ALARM

People respected Frances for her hard work and determination.

When Franklin Delano Roosevelt became governor of New York in 1928, he asked her to run the state's labor office.

On November 4, 1932, Roosevelt was elected president.

It was a difficult time. The country had plunged into the Great Depression. Millions of Americans lost their jobs. Children went hungry.

The person Roosevelt chose to be Secretary of Labor would face enormous challenges.

No woman in American history had served in a president's cabinet.

But one day Frances received a call: Roosevelt wished to see her.

Frances could guess what he wanted to ask. And she was ready.

Whenever Frances had an idea about how to make things better, she scribbled it on a small slip of paper. Then she stuck it in the lower right-hand drawer of her desk.

Now she pulled out those slips to make a long list of her bold ideas for change.

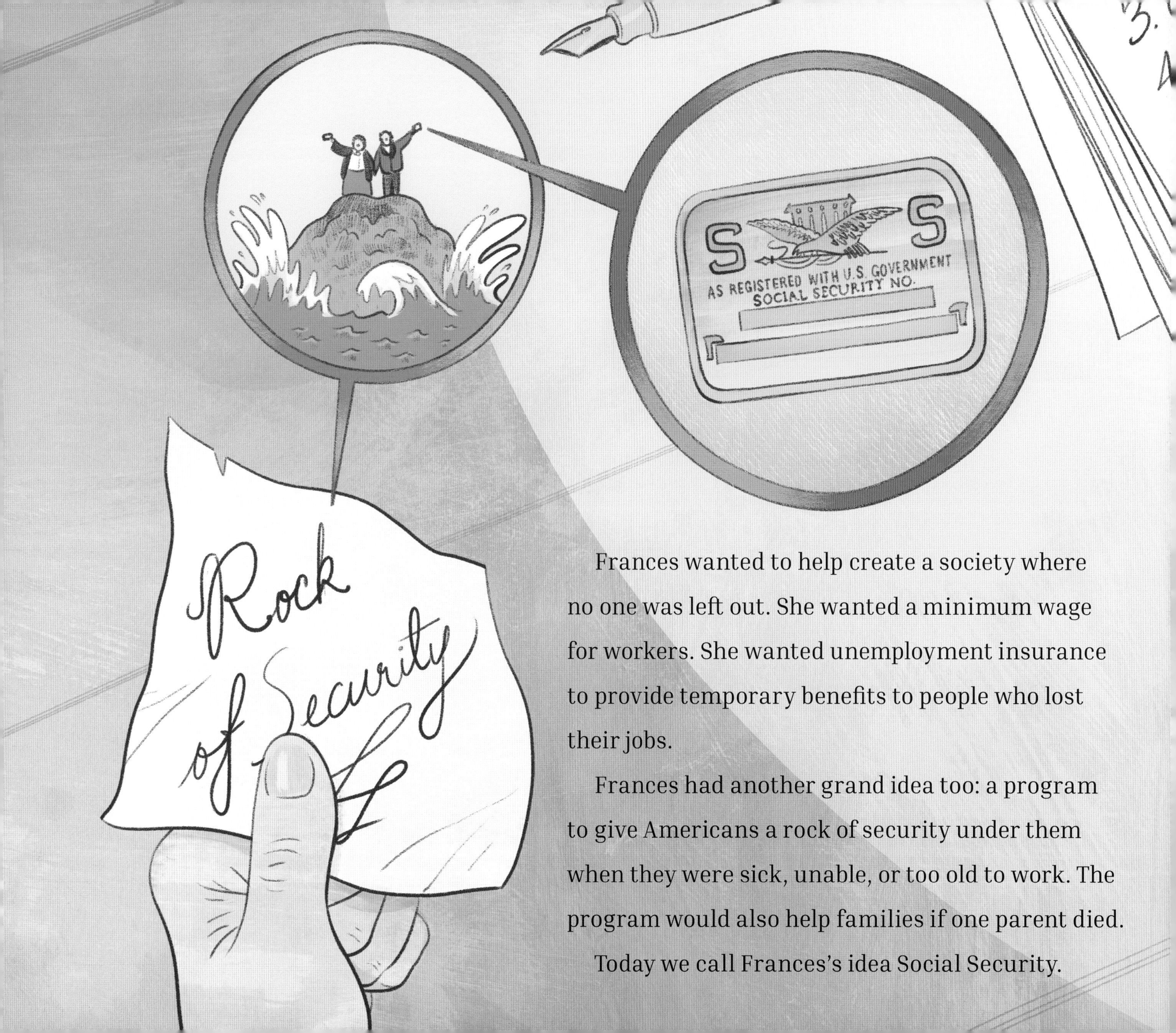

Frances wanted to help create a society where no one was left out. She wanted a minimum wage for workers. She wanted unemployment insurance to provide temporary benefits to people who lost their jobs.

Frances had another grand idea too: a program to give Americans a rock of security under them when they were sick, unable, or too old to work. The program would also help families if one parent died.

Today we call Frances's idea Social Security.

Roosevelt listened to her ideas and wondered if they could all be done. He told her, "You have to invent the way to do these things."

And that is exactly what Frances did.

It wasn't easy for Frances to move from New York to Washington. Her husband was ill and often in the hospital. Although her daughter, Susanna, was now a teenager, Frances often had to leave her in the care of others.

But Frances knew she had to try to make things better not only in her own time—but for generations far into the future.

When Frances Perkins set about to change history, she did it the best way she knew how—little by little, step by step, using her heart and her mind.

She listened to ideas, gave speeches, made plans, and gathered people to work with her.

The process was long and complicated.

Once, to meet a deadline, Frances invited committee members to her house and locked the door until they finished their work at two in the morning.

Social Security was one part of President Roosevelt's New Deal to help America recover from the depression. He signed the Social Security Act into law on August 14, 1935.

Frances was standing right there.

Today, Social Security provides help for survivors: the children or spouse of a worker who has passed away. It supports children and adults with disabilities. The program also benefits older people who've paid Social Security taxes during their working lives.

Through Social Security, we've built a society where we help one another. An idea that began as a slip of paper in Frances Perkins's desk has become a vital part of our democracy.

Now back to those math questions. Although it might well change in the future, right now most people can begin receiving Social Security benefits as early as—you guessed it—age sixty-two.

So whether you benefit from Social Security now or on some far-off day, think of this dedicated public servant and remember to say, "Thanks, Frances!"

Now, Back to Those Math Questions

Maybe you've never heard of Social Security. Or perhaps you already know about the Social Security program because you and your family receive payments. These payments are called benefits. The Social Security program helps Americans of all ages.

There are three main areas of Social Security.

- The children and spouse of a worker who has died can often receive what are called survivor benefits.

- Another part of the program helps children and adults with disabilities. Disability benefits provide income for children, as well as for adults who cannot work.

- Social Security also helps people in retirement by providing income benefits. Now, if you're reading this book and you're younger than ten, it might be hard to imagine yourself old enough to retire.

We began with two math questions for young readers.

1. How many years will it be until you turn sixty-two? If you can do this arithmetic problem yourself, you subtract your age from the number 62. Or you can ask someone to help you find the answer.

2. What year will that be? Then, to find out what year that will be, the next step is to add that number to whatever year it is when you are reading this book. Although people do many different kinds of jobs, and stop working at different ages, we can all benefit from saving money for a time when we might not be able to support ourselves.

Now, it's not possible to know if the Social Security program will be the same when you reach retirement age or if you need to depend on Social Security benefits for other reasons, such as being disabled.

But, in general, Social Security is something that is part of our entire working lives. Most employers will take out some part of a worker's pay for Social Security taxes. When we pay Social Security taxes, that money flows out to people who need benefits now for a variety of reasons. Later, when we need the benefits, the money comes from people paying the taxes too. It is a program that makes us all a stronger nation.

We can thank Frances Perkins for caring about people's lives and wanting Americans to feel secure. Just as we learn reading, math, social studies, and science, understanding how money works in our lives and society is important. This is called economic education.

You will face decisions about money long before you are ready to retire.

If you receive a gift of money or an allowance, should you spend it or save it? How long will it take to save for a special pair of shoes or a bicycle?

Some decisions about money are small; others are big. Today you might need to decide whether to spend or save a dollar. In the future, you might have to decide how much money to borrow to go to college or buy a car. Perhaps someday you will want to start a family or save money to purchase a home.

One thing is certain: the more we know, the better choices we can make.

THANKS, FRANCES!

President Franklin D. Roosevelt signs the Social Security Act on August 14, 1935. Pictured behind him: Representative Robert Doughton, Senator Robert Wagner, Representative John Dingell, Representative Joshua Twing Brooks, Secretary of Labor Frances Perkins, and Senator Pat Harrison.

Author's Note

Frances Perkins devoted her life to social justice and public service. She was born in Massachusetts on April 10, 1880. After graduating from Mount Holyoke College in 1902, Frances (whose nickname was Fanny and who was sometimes called Perk by her college friends) worked and taught in Chicago, where she was inspired by the work of legendary social activist Jane Addams, founder of Hull House. In 1910, Frances received a master's degree from Columbia University. After witnessing the Triangle Waist Company fire on March 25, 1911, she turned her attention to workplace safety and reform. Frances went to work as executive secretary of the Committee on Safety, which created a legislative panel called the New York State Factory Investigating Commission. Frances's investigative efforts helped the Commission pass new laws to protect workers. She married Paul Wilson in 1913 and was the mother of one daughter, Susanna.

Frances continued to work on labor issues under New York governors Alfred E. Smith and Franklin D. Roosevelt. In 1933, she became the first woman appointed to a presidential cabinet when newly elected President Franklin D. Roosevelt named her Secretary of Labor. Frances held the position for twelve years (1933–1945), becoming the longest serving Secretary in history.

During the difficult years of the Great Depression, Frances helped President Roosevelt implement significant social reforms to benefit Americans, called the "New Deal." Many of the rights and programs that benefit working Americans today were established at this time, including minimum wage, unemployment insurance, Social Security, and survivor benefits. Frances helped to set restrictions on child labor, as well as rules governing industry safety, minimum wages, and maximum work weeks.

Frances Perkins died on May 14, 1965. Her home in Maine has been preserved as the Frances Perkins Center.

Frances Perkins at work for the Factory Investigation Commission, circa 1911.

Learn More

Frances Perkins Center
www.francesperkinscenter.org/resources

Honoring the Achievements of FDR's Secretary of Labor Franklin D. Roosevelt Presidential Library
www.fdrlibrary.org/perkins

Frances Perkins's Oral History
Columbia University's Notable New Yorkers
www.columbia.edu/cu/lweb/digital/collections/nny/perkinsf/introduction.html

The Roots of Social Security: text and audio excerpts from a 1962 speech given by Frances Perkins
Social Security Administration
www.ssa.gov/history/perkins5.html

A Short Bio of Frances Perkins
Social Security Administration
www.ssa.gov/history/fpbiossa.html

The 1911 Triangle Waist Company Fire
Cornell University's Kheel Center
trianglefire.ilr.cornell.edu

Hear Frances Perkins speak here: *trianglefire.ilr.cornell.edu/primary/lectures/FrancesPerkinsLecture.html?CFID=2274790&CFTOKEN=10773700*

Frances Perkins and Jewish Refugees from the Holocaust United States Holocaust Memorial Museum
encyclopedia.ushmm.org/content/en/article/frances-perkins

Social Security and You
Social Security Administration
www.ssa.gov/people/parents

Detailed Chronology of Social Insurance & Social Security
Social Security Administration
www.ssa.gov/history/chrono.html

Economic Education for Parents, Teachers, & Scouts
The Federal Reserve Bank of St. Louis
www.stlouisfed.org/education/parent-resources
www.stlouisfed.org/education/teacher-professional-development
www.stlouisfed.org/education/girl-scout-activities

Photo Credits

page 37
Library of Congress Prints and Photographs division, LC-USZ62-123278

page 38
Frances Perkins Papers, Rare Book and Manuscript Library, Columbia University

page 40
Library of Congress Prints and Photographs division, LC-USZ62-123275

Bibliography

Downey, Kirstin. The Woman Behind the New Deal: The Life and Legacy of Frances Perkins—Social Security, Unemployment Insurance, and the Minimum Wage.
New York: Anchor Books, 2010.

Perkins, Frances. The Roosevelt I Knew.
New York: Penguin, 2011. First published in 1946.

Frances Perkins Oral History. Columbia University Notable New Yorkers project.
www.columbia.edu/cu/lweb/digital/collections/nny/perkinsf/introduction.html

Frances Perkins, 1918

Source Notes

"Too much blood has been spilled..."
Schneiderman, R. Jewish Women's Archive.
www.jwa.org/media/excerpt-from-rose-schneidermans-april-2-1911-speech

"inquires, penetrates, goes to the bottom of things..."
Perkins, F. Oral History. Columbia University Libraries Oral History Research Office, Notable New Yorkers, Part 1, Session 1, p. 37.

"a turning point..."
www.francesperkinscenter.org/life-new

"You have to invent..."
ibid., Part 3, Session 1, p. 597.